A Kid's Guide to Drawing America™

How to Draw
Connecticut's
Sights and Symbols

Jennifer Quasha

Rockwell Media Center
Whittlesey Drive
Bethel, CT 06801

The Rosen Publishing Group's
PowerKids Press™
New York

To Goss and John

Published in 2002 by The Rosen Publishing Group, Inc.
29 East 21st Street, New York, NY 10010

First Edition

Book and Layout Design: Kim Sonsky
Project Editor: Jannell Khu

Illustration Credits: Jamie Grecco
Photo Credits: p. 7 © Joseph Sohm; Visions of America/CORBIS; p. 8 (photo) courtesy of the Florence Griswold Museum, Lyme Historical Society Archives; p. 8 (sketch) courtesy of the Florence Griswold Museum; p. 9 (painting) courtesy of the Florence Griswold Museum; pp. 12, 14 © One Mile Up, Incorporated; p. 16 © David Muench/CORBIS; p. 18 © Roger Tidman/CORBIS; p. 20 © Gary Braasch/CORBIS; pp. 22, 28 © Index Stock; p. 24 © Mark Gibson/CORBIS; p. 26 © Hiroya Minakuchi/Seapics.com/Innerpsace Visions.

Quasha, Jennifer
How to draw Connecticut's sights and symbols / Jennifer Quasha.
p. cm. — (A kid's guide to drawing America)
Includes index.
Summary: This book explains how to draw some of Connecticut's sights and symbols, including the state seal, the official flower, and the official state ship.
  ISBN 0-8239-6061-7
1. Emblems, State—Connecticut—Juvenile literature 2. Connecticut in art—Juvenile literature 3. Drawing—Technique—Juvenile literature [1. Emblems, State—Connecticut 2. Connecticut 3. Drawing—Technique]
I. Title II. Series
  2001
  743'.8'09746—dc21

Manufactured in the United States of America

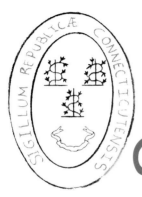

CONTENTS

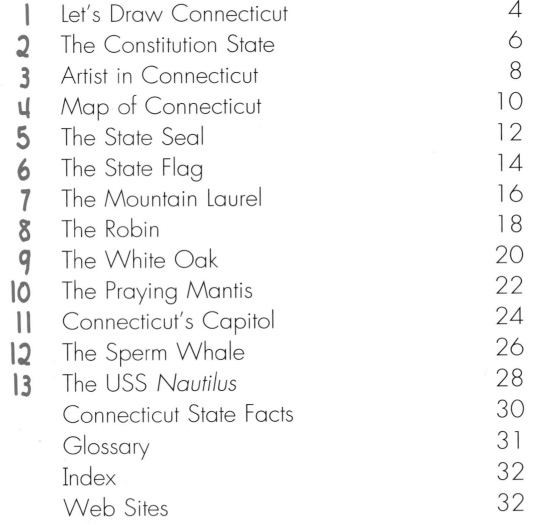

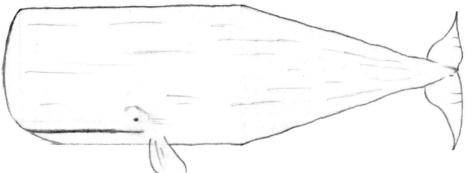

Let's Draw Connecticut

Connecticut is one of the oldest states in the northeast United States, and it was one of the original thirteen colonies. Early residents of Connecticut produced copper coins, rubber shoes, friction matches, and many other products that are similar to ones we use today.

Connecticut is proud of Eli Whitney, the inventor of the cotton gin. Whitney came up with a method of mass production in a factory in Hamden, Connecticut, in the early 1800s. Citizens of Connecticut have invented and produced many products, such as the first submarine, the first portable typewriter, and even the first collapsible toothpaste tube!

Connecticut is home to many industries, including transportation, electrical equipment, machinery, publishing, scientific instruments, and metal products. Its most famous industry is insurance. Connecticut is sometimes known as the Insurance State because many forms of modern insurance, such as life, accident, and health insurance, were started there. It also has a rich agricultural trade and produces dairy products, eggs, poultry, timber, and other nursery products.

The state's official symbols illustrate Connecticut's rich history, which dates all the way from the early 1600s. You can learn more about Connecticut's sights and symbols, and how to draw them, with this book. The drawings begin with a simple shape, then you add other shapes. Under every drawing, directions explain how to do the step. Also, each new step of the drawing is shown in red to help guide you. You can also check out the drawing terms for help.

You will need the following supplies to draw Connecticut's sights and symbols:

- A sketch pad
- An eraser
- A number 2 pencil
- A pencil sharpener

These are some of the shapes and drawing terms you need to know to draw Connecticut's sights and symbols:

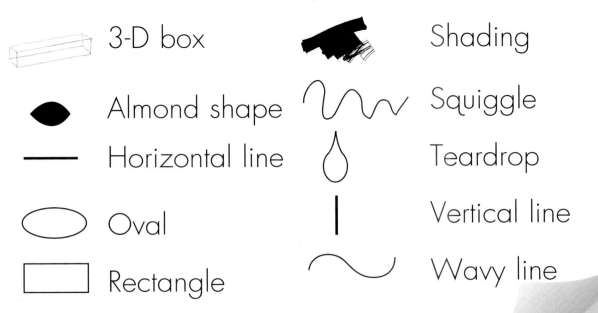

3-D box

Shading

Almond shape

Squiggle

Horizontal line

Teardrop

Oval

Vertical line

Rectangle

Wavy line

The Constitution State

On January 9, 1788, Connecticut became the fifth state to join the Union. Connecticut covers 5,544 square miles (14,359 sq km) of land and has a population of more than 3,000,000 people. About 133,000 people live in Hartford, the capital of Connecticut. The city of Bridgeport has the largest population, with more than 137,000 people.

In its earliest colonial days, Connecticut attempted to establish a political plan for the kind of government it wanted. This resulted in the Fundamental Orders of 1639, written by Thomas Hooker, John Haynes, and Roger Ludlow. When the U.S. Constitution was written in the early 1780s, the Fundamental Orders of 1639 was used as a model. This was how Connecticut earned its nickname, the Constitution State. Connecticut is also called the Nutmeg State because its early settlers sold objects carved out of the wood of the nutmeg tree.

The Constitution of the United States was signed on September 17, 1787, in Philadelphia, Pennsylvania. Connecticut's Fundamental Orders of 1639 was used as a model for the Constitution.

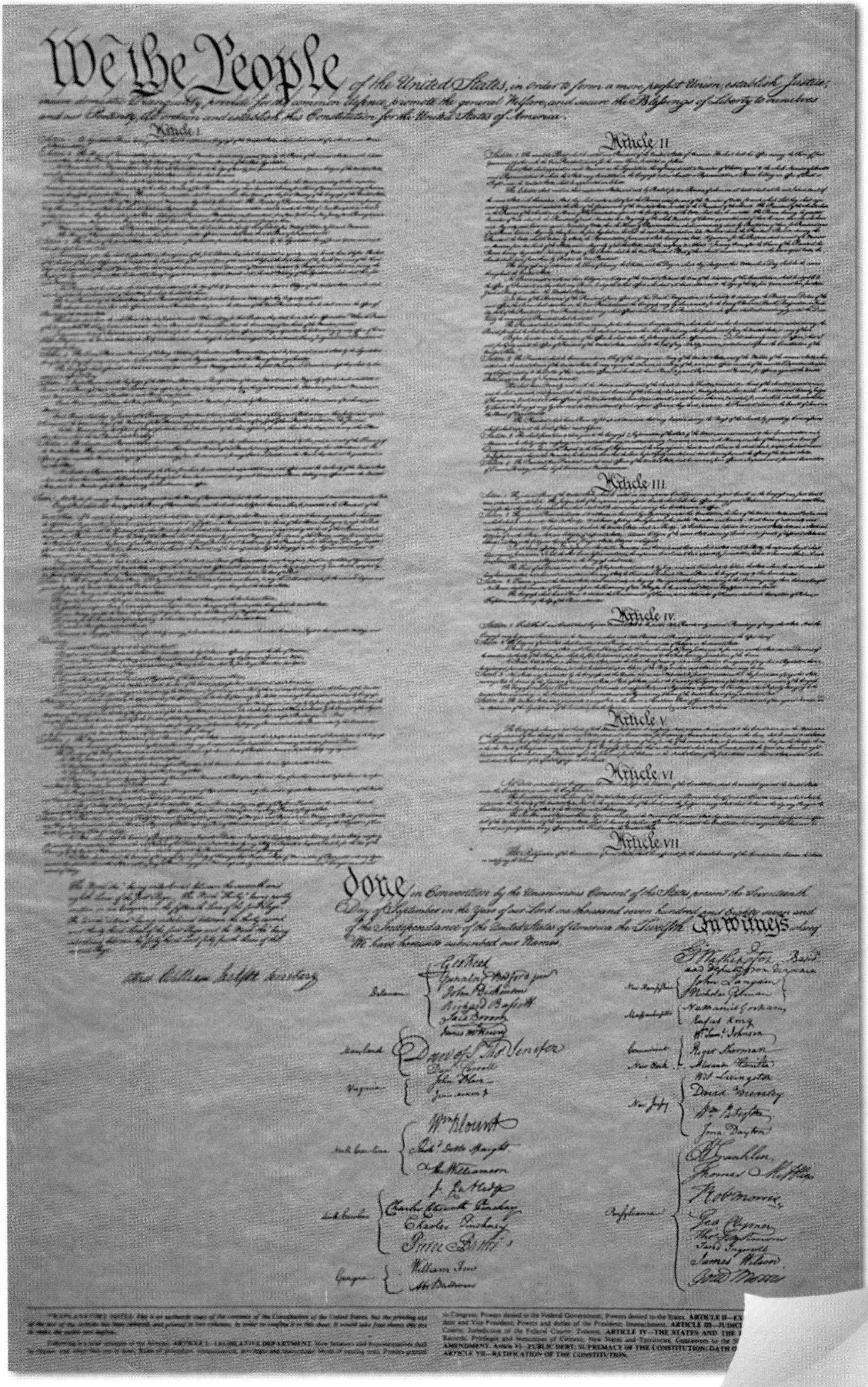

Artist in Connecticut

This photograph shows Henry Ward Ranger painting outdoors.

Landscape painter Henry Ward Ranger was born in Syracuse, New York, in 1858. From 1873 to 1875, Ranger attended Syracuse University's College of Fine Arts, where his father taught photography. He quit school before earning his degree, to help in his father's studio. He began painting watercolors, and by 1881, he showed his work at the American Watercolor Society. In the mid-1880s, Ranger studied in France and the Netherlands. He liked the masters of the French Barbizon School, including Jean-Baptiste Camille Corot (1796–1875) and Narcisse Virgile Diaz de la Pena (1807–1876). The Barbizon School was a

This is a landscape sketch from one of Ranger's sketchbooks. It was done in graphite on paper.

group of painters who painted landscapes and worked in the village of Barbizon, near Paris. In 1887, Ranger showed his paintings at the National Academy of Design in New York. In 1888, he returned to the United States to live in New York City. While traveling through the Connecticut town of Old Lyme, Ranger fell in love with the town's beautiful landscape. In 1899, he and some friends founded an artists' colony there. Many of Ranger's works convey a sense of nature's beauty and mystery. Ranger died in 1916, but he is remembered for his New England landscapes, such as *Groton Long Point*, an oil painting he completed in 1910.

Groton Long Point was painted by Ranger in 1910. The work was painted in oil on canvas and measures 36" x 28" (91.4 cm X 71.1 cm).

Map of Connecticut

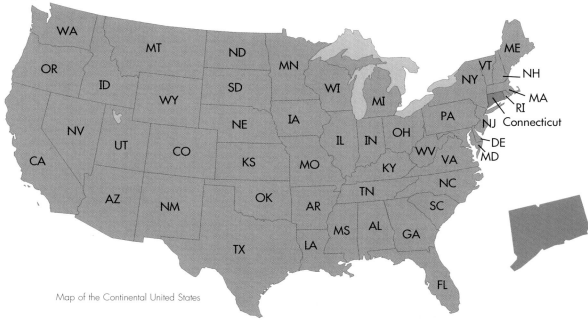

Map of the Continental United States

    Connecticut is the third-smallest state in America. Its eastern, northern, and western borders are next to Rhode Island, Massachusetts, and New York, in that order. Its southern border stretches along the Long Island Sound. Connecticut got its name from the Connecticut River, which flows through the center of the state. The name Connecticut comes from the Native American word *quinnehtukqut*, which means "beside the long, tidal river."

    Mount Fissel, which measures 2,380 feet (725 m), is the highest point in Connecticut. The state's topography, or the shapes and forms of the land, is made up of coastal plains, flat central valleys, and hills covered with hardwood forests.

1

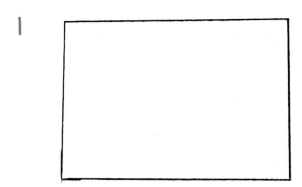

Start by drawing a rectangle.

2

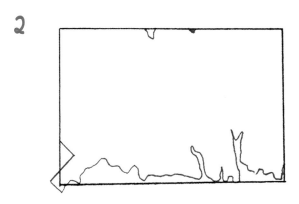

Using the rectangle as a guide, draw the shape of Connecticut.

3

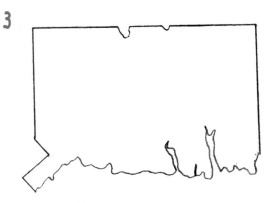

Erase extra lines.

4

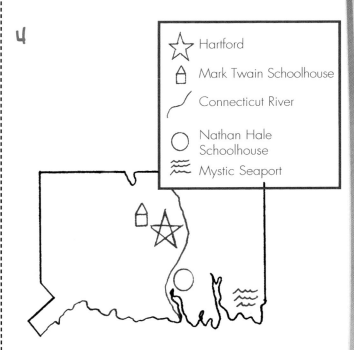

a. Draw in Mystic Seaport, using three wavy lines.
b. Show the Nathan Hale Schoolhouse by drawing a circle.
c. Use a square and a triangle to draw the Mark Twain Schoolhouse.
d. Use a wavy line to draw the Connecticut River.
e. Draw a star to mark Connecticut's capital, Hartford.
f. To finish your map, draw a key in the upper-right corner to mark the state's points of interest.

The State Seal

The Connecticut state seal, adopted in 1931, is similar to the state flag because like the flag, in the center of the seal there are three grapevines with ripe grapes. Underneath the vines is a banner that includes the state motto. The grapevines represent the first English settlements in Connecticut, which moved down from Massachusetts in the 1630s. Those settlers picked up and moved like grapevines that were transplanted. Before the American Revolution, the inscription around the state seal read "SIGILL. REIP. CONNECTICUTENSIS." In 1784, the words on the seal were spelled out instead of being shortened. The inscription became *SIGILLUM REIPUBLICAE CONNECTICUTENSIS*, which in Latin means "the Seal of the State of Connecticut."

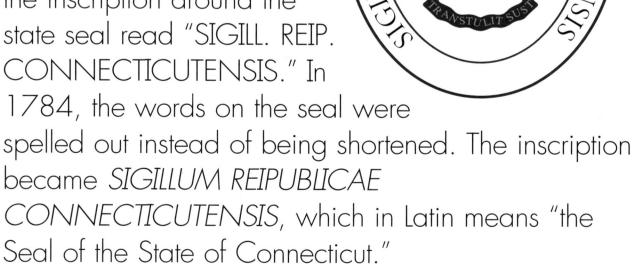

1

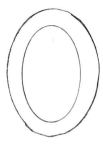

Start by drawing two ovals.

2

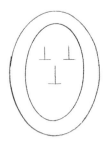

Draw three upside-down *T*'s.

3

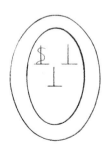

Draw a wavy line in the shape of an *S* over one of the upside-down *T*'s.

4

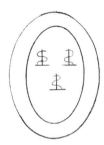

Draw a wavy line in the shape of a backward *S* over the next two upside-down *T*'s.

5

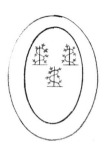

Add tiny leaves and grapes to each *S* shape.

6

Draw an upside down *V* and an arc.

7

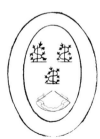

Use this as a guide to draw the banner as shown.

8

Erase extra lines. To finish your seal, just write in the letters.

13

The State Flag

Connecticut Governor O. Vincent Coffin proposed a state flag on May 29, 1895, and in 1897, the state flag was approved. The flag is 5 ½ feet (1.68 m) long and 4 ⅓ feet (1.32 m) wide. The flag is azure blue, or the deep blue color of an unclouded sky. In the center is a white rococo shield with gold details. Rococo is a style of art that was popular in the eighteenth century. Rococo art had many details and decorations, just like the shield within the flag. Inside the shield are three grapevines with purple grapes. Underneath the shield is a banner with the Connecticut state motto, *qui transtulit sustinet*. These Latin words mean He Who Transplanted Still Sustains. The flag is trimmed with a gold-and-brown border.

1

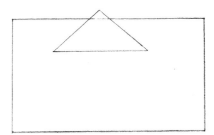

Start by drawing a large rectangle and adding a wide triangle.

2

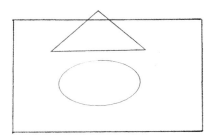

Draw an oval under the triangle.

3

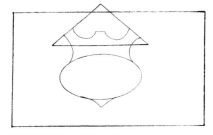

Using the oval and triangle as a guide, draw the shape of the crest inside the flag.

4

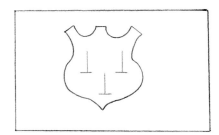

Erase extra lines and draw three upside-down *T*'s.

5

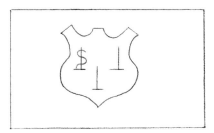

Draw a wavy line in the shape of an *S* over one of the upside-down *T*'s.

6

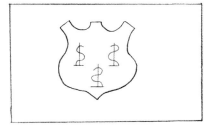

Draw a wavy line in the shape of a backward *S* over the next two upside-down *T*'s.

7

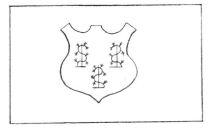

Add tiny leaves and grapes to each *S* shape and your flag is complete.

15

The Mountain Laurel

Connecticut accepted the mountain laurel as its official state flower on April 17, 1907. The blossoms of the mountain laurel are pink and white and grow in bunches. Their leaves are wide and also grow in groups. Mountain laurels, also known as calico bush and spoonwood, have a beautiful smell that has attracted many admirers, including the first colonists who came to America. In 1624, John Smith, who lived in the first English settlement of Jamestown, wrote about the mountain laurel in his *General History of Virginia*. Native Americans called the wood of the mountain laurel "spoonwood" because eating utensils often were made from its wood.

1

Draw a large circle and a small circle.

2

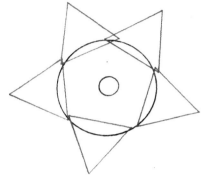

Add five triangles around the large circle.

3

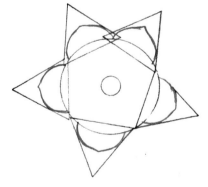

Draw the shape of the flower's petals inside each triangle.

4

Erase any extra lines.

5

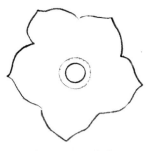

Add another circle around the small circle.

6

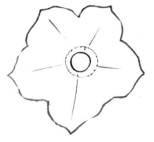

Add one line inside the center of each petal.

7

Add shading and detail and your flower is complete.

The Robin

The robin became Connecticut's state bird in 1943. The robin belongs to a group of birds called thrushes. English colonists gave the robin its name because it reminded them of a bird in England called a robin redbreast. Male robins are mostly a brownish gray color with a red underbelly. The female robin has no red breast and is a duller color of the same brownish gray. Robins are about 8–9 inches (20–23 cm) long, with a 4-inch (10-cm) tail. Female robins lay either three or four blue eggs. Once the eggs hatch, the male robin cares for the brood while the female prepares for another. Robins eat beetles, caterpillars, spiders, earthworms, and snails. If you happen to spot a robin, you may get a chance to hear its beautiful song.

1

Draw three circles, noting their placement on the page.

2

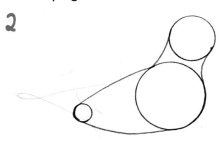

Connect your circles to form the bird's body and head.

3

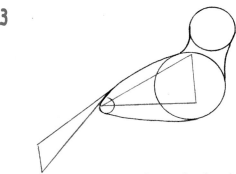

Use two triangles to draw the bird's tail and wing.

4

Shape the body and erase extra lines.

5

Use thin rectangles and lines to form the bird's legs and feet.

6

Add a thin triangle for the bird's beak, erase extra lines, and add the bird's eye.

7

Add shading and detail and your bird is complete.

19

The White Oak

Connecticut adopted the white oak as its official state tree on April 16, 1947. The white oak is a large tree that can grow 60–100 feet (18.3–30.5 m) tall with branches that can spread 60 feet (18.3 m) wide. Oaks can live for 350–400 years! An oak tree's trunk is covered with a light-gray, scaly bark and its leaves are shiny and green. In the fall, the leaves turn deep red. Oak trees have acorn seeds that are eaten by animals such as deer, squirrels, and chipmunks. The English colonists used oak wood to build houses. The USS *Constitution*, Connecticut's official state ship until 1983, also was built with white oak. Today people still use oak to make furniture.

1

Draw a thin rectangle for the trunk of the tree.

2

Add five thin triangles to the top area of the trunk for branches.

3

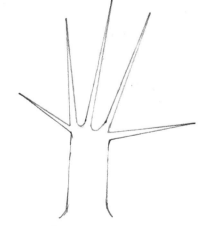

Erase any extra lines.

4

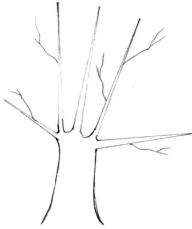

Now draw curvy lines from your triangle branches. The more you add, the fuller your tree will look.

5

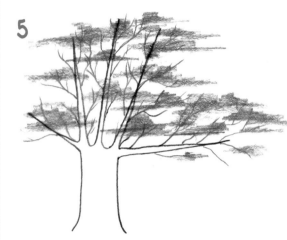

Add leaves by lightly using the side of your pencil to shade the branches.

6

Add detail by shading the trunk of the tree and your tree is complete.

The Praying Mantis

The praying mantis became Connecticut's official insect on October 1, 1977, even though it is not native to the state. Praying mantises originally came from Africa, Europe, and Asia. They can only be found in Connecticut during warm spring and summer months because they die in cold weather. The praying mantis got its name because of how it looks and behaves. The praying mantis can remain completely still with its two large front legs raised together, similar to how a person might look when praying. In Greek, the word *mantis* means prophet or diviner. Praying mantises are about 2–2.5 inches (5–6.4 cm) long and are green or brown. They have four hind legs and two large front legs. They eat flies, grasshoppers, caterpillars, moths, and sometimes other mantises!

1

Start by drawing a triangle for the mantis' head.

2

Now add a rectangle and two circles for the body.

3

Connect your circles and add two smaller circles on the mantis' head for eyes.

4

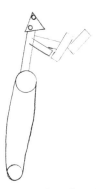

Now add four rectangles for the top set of the mantis' legs.

5

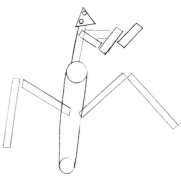

Add another four rectangles for the mantis' middle set of legs.

6

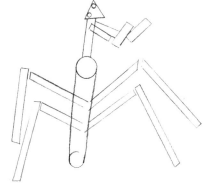

Add another four rectangles for the mantis' bottom set of legs.

7

Erase your extra lines, and add curved lines to the ends of each leg.

8

Add shading and detail and your mantis is complete.

23

Connecticut's Capitol

In 1878, the state capitol of Connecticut was built in Hartford. The building was designed by Richard M. Upjohn. It has 26 Gothic arches with carved-out spaces for pieces of sculpture. The building also has tympana, or carved scenes, above the portals. Each side of the building was designed to feature a piece of Connecticut's history. For example, the front of the building has six statues of Connecticut's historical figures. One statue is of William Buckingham, who was Connecticut's governor during the Civil War years. There is also a statue of Nathan Hale, the official state hero and an important figure in the Revolutionary War. The Connecticut state capitol building became a national historic landmark in 1971.

24

1

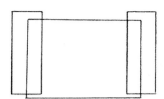

Start by drawing three rectangles, noting their placement on the page.

2

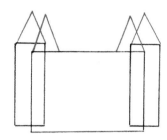

Now draw four triangles on your rectangles as shown. Erase extra lines.

3

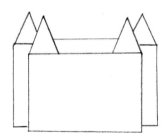

Connect your bottom two rectangles by drawing a straight line between them and the triangles.

4

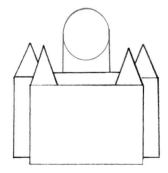

Add two straight lines and a circle for the building's dome.

5

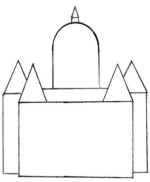

Erase extra lines. Add a small rectangle and a triangle on top of the dome.

6

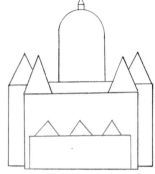

To make the front entrance, draw a rectangle and three triangles as shown.

7

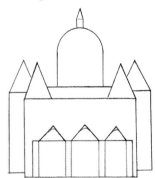

Draw three rectangles for columns.

8

You can add windows using squares and rectangles. Erase extra lines and smudges, add detail, and you're done.

The Sperm Whale

In 1975, the sperm whale became Connecticut's state animal. During the 1800s, Connecticut had the second-largest whaling industry after Massachusetts. Whales were hunted mainly for their sperm oil, which was used to make soap, candles, cosmetic creams, and as fuel to burn in lamps. Today the sperm whale is an endangered species.

The sperm whale can grow to be 60 feet (18.3 m) long and is the largest of the toothed whales. The sperm whale also has the biggest brain of all animals. Sperm whales have a large, square head and a dark body with wrinkly skin. They can dive for up to 1 hour! Sperm whales eat squid and cuttlefish and can dive down 3,000 feet (914 m) to find their meals.

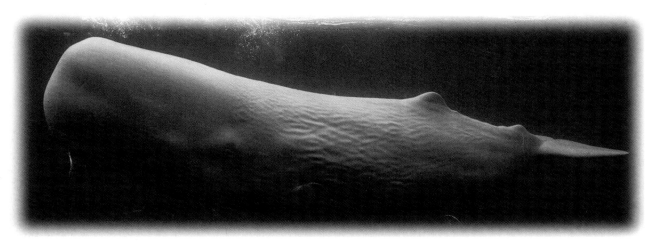

1

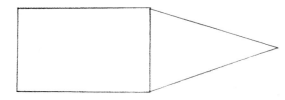

Start by drawing a rectangle for the whale's body.

2

Add a triangle to complete the shape of the body.

3

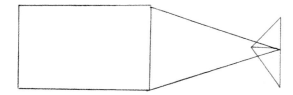

Add two small triangles to the end of the larger one to make the whale's tail.

4

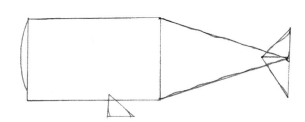

Draw a small triangle for the whale's flipper. Add a curved line for the nose and wavy lines for the tail.

5

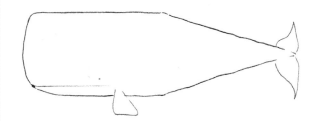

Erase any extra lines and smudges.

6

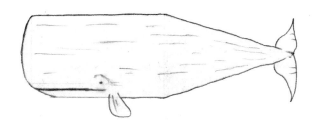

Add detail and shading to complete your sperm whale.

The USS *Nautilus*

The USS *Nautilus* has been Connecticut's official state ship since 1983. The USS *Nautilus* was built over an 18-month period between 1952 and 1954. The USS *Nautilus* was to be a part of the U.S. Navy, and it was the world's first nuclear-powered submarine. The sub was 323 feet (98 m) long and had a crew of 104 people. It had a top speed of 22 knots (41 km/hr) on the surface of the water and 23 knots (43 km/hr) underneath the water. On June 14, 1952, President Harry S. Truman lowered the submarine into the sea. The submarine logged more than 500,000 miles (804,672 km) and was used for more than 20 years. Today it is berthed next to the Submarine Force Library in Groton, Connecticut.

1

Start by drawing two circles, the larger one on the right and the smaller one on the left.

2

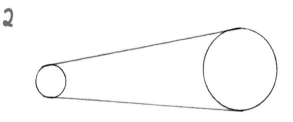

Connect the two circles to draw the outline of the submarine.

3

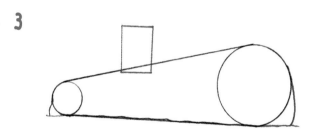

Add a rectangle to the top of the submarine and a wavy line to the bottom of the submarine.

4

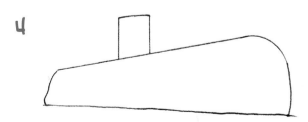

Erase extra lines and smudges.

5

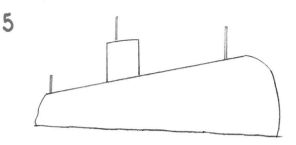

Add three thin rectangles for flagpoles.

6

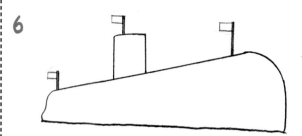

Add three small rectangles for flags.

7

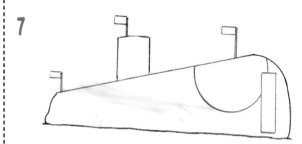

To draw the flags draped over the front of the submarine, use a half circle and a rectangle.

8

To complete the submarine, use squares for windows, and shading to add depth. You even can draw the flags and people on deck.

29

Connecticut State Facts

Statehood	January 9, 1788, 5th state
Area	5,544 square miles (14,359 sq km)
Population	3,282,000
Capital	Hartford, population, 133,100
Most Populated City	Bridgeport, population, 138,000
Industries	Insurance, transportation, machinery, publishing, scientific instruments, metal
Agriculture	Dairy products, eggs, poultry, trees
Motto	He Who Transplanted Still Sustains
Song	"Yankee Doodle"
Flower	Mountain laurel
Bird	Robin
Tree	White oak
Insect	Praying mantis
Animal	Sperm whale
Ship	USS *Nautilus*
Composer	Charles Edward Ives
Fossil	*Eubrontes giganteus* (dinosaur)
Hero	Nathan Hale
Mineral	Garnet
Shellfish	Eastern oyster
Nicknames	The Constitution State, The Nutmeg State

Glossary

admirers (ad-MYR-urz) People who value someone or something a great deal.

American Revolution (uh-MER-un-ken reh-vuh-LOO-shun) Battles that soldiers from the colonies fought against England for freedom.

berthed (BERTHD) Docked.

Civil War (SIH-vul WOR) The war fought between the northern and southern states of America from 1861 to 1865.

endangered species (en-DAYN-jerd SPEE-sheez) Species, or kinds of wild animals, that will probably die out if we don't protect them.

Gothic (GAH-thik) A style of architecture popular from the twelfth to the early sixteenth century.

inscription (in-SKRIHP-shun) Writing on an object, like a coin or dollar bill.

insurance (in-SHUR-ints) Protection against loss or damage.

landmark (LAND-mark) An important building, structure, or place.

mass production (MAS proh-DUK-shun) The process of making things in large quantities.

motto (MAH-toh) A short sentence or phrase that says what someone believes or what something stands for.

nursery (NUR-suh-ree) A place where plants and trees are raised and sold.

portals (POR-tulz) Doors or entrances.

residents (REH-zih-dents) People who live in a certain town or city.

rococo (roh-KOH-ko) A style of art that was popular in the eighteenth century and that had many details and decorations.

species (SPEE-sheez) A single kind of plant or animal.

sustains (suh-STAYNZ) Keeps going.

topography (tuh-PAH-gruh-fee) A way of describing the shape of different landmasses, such as the height of mountains.

transplanted (TRANZ-plant-id) Moved from one place to another.

tympana (TIM-puh-nuh) Space under a building's arches.

utensils (yoo-TEN-silz) Tools that are useful in doing or making something.

Index

Web Sites

For more information about Connecticut, check out these
    Web sites:
www.chs.org/
www.kids.state.ct.us